Addresses

AT THE

INAUGURATION OF

ALLEN R. BENTON,

As Chancellor of the

University of Nebraska.

WEDNESDAY, SEPTEMBER 6, 1871.

FOR THE UNIVERSITY.

LINCOLN, NEBRASKA:
STATESMAN POWER PRESS JOB PRINT.
1871.

Order of Exercises.

September 6, 1871.

AFTERNOON.

Music.

Prayer.
By Rev. L. B. Fifield.

Music.

Induction into office.
By Acting Governor W. H. James,
President of the Board of Regents.

Music.

Inaugural Address.
By Chancellor Benton.

Music.

Benediction.
By Rev. O. T. Conger.

EVENING.

Music.

Prayer.
By Rev. H. P. Peck.

University Address.
By Hon. J. Sterling Morton.

Music.

Benediction.
By Chancellor Benton.

In accordance with previous announcement the Inauguration of ALLEN R. BENTON, A.M., L.L.D., as Chancellor of the University of Nebraska, took place at two o'clock September 6, 1871, in the large and beautiful Chapel of the University.

The desk of the Chapel was decorated with large and fragrant boquets of flowers. The day was unusually fine and a very large concourse crowded the Chapel both afternoon and evening. The music for the afternoon was furnished by Mr. S. B. HOHMAN, assisted by Mr. and Mrs. J. H. ALFORD, Mrs, G. A. RANDALL and Dr. W. W. WARDNER.

According to a previous resolution, the Board of Regents adjourned to attend the inaugural exercises of the University. A little after two o'clock the Board of Regents, the Faculty, and invited visitors, proceeded in a body from the Regents' room to the Chapel of the University and were seated on the platform.

Acting Governor WM. H. JAMES, President of the Board of Regents, who presided on the occasion, announced that the exercises would be epened with music. The choir then sang "How beautiful are thy dwellings," after which the Rev. L. B. FIFIELD pronounced a fervent and appropriate prayer, invoking the Divine blessing on the new University, the Chancellor, the Students, and the State.

The Chancellor was then inducted into office by the President of the Board who delivered an address [see the address page 4,] and presented the Chancellor-elect with the keys of the University.

To this address of Acting Governor JAMES, Chancellor BENTON, who had remained standing, replied in a few words, accepting the trust. [See page 5.]

After music, "Columbia's Call," the Chancellor proceeded to deliver his Inaugural Address. At its conclusion the choir sung "Farewell," and the Rev. O. T. CONGER pronounced the benediction.

Evening Exercises.

In the evening the Chapel was again crowded to listen to the "University Address," delivered by the Hon. J. STERLING MORTON.

Music was furnished by Messrs. HOHMAN, OAKLEY, WHEELER, LATHROP, WHITE and NORTHROP.

After the music the REV. H. P. PECK offered an impressive and eloquent invocation of Divine blessings on all the interests of the University.

The HON. MR. MORTON was then introduced by the President of the Board, and delivered the University Address. [See Address in proper place.]

REGENT J. B. MAXFIELD, on behalf of the Board, set forth in earnest words the duty of the citizens of Lincoln toward the University.

CHANCELLOR BENTON then read letters from distinguished gentlemen from abroad: IRA MAYHEW, GEO. H. PENDLETON, WM. BROSS. [See last page.]

Benediction by CHANCELLOR BENTON.

On the return of the Board of Regents to their room, REGENT C. S. CHASE offered the following resolution, which was adopted:

Resolved, That the Board solicit for publication, a copy of the Inaugural Address of CHANCELLOR BENTON; also a copy of the University Address of the HON. J. STERLING MORTON, and that one thousand copies be published in pamphlet form under the supervision of the University Committee, together with a sketch of the inaugural exercises, and that the Secretary solicit copies of the several addresses on behalf of the Board.

Thus closed the interesting and impressive ceremonies, inaugurating the first Chancellor, and the work of the new University of Nebraska.

ADDRESS OF GOVERNOR W. H. JAMES,

President of Board of Regents,

—AND—

Reply of CHANCELLOR BENTON.

CHANCELLOR BENTON:

In assuming the position allotted to me in the opening and dedicatory exercises of our State University, it will doubtless be expected of me that I should express some sentiments congratulatory on its doors being thrown wide open to the youth of our young and growing Commonwealth. But with few words, I shall leave this task to other and abler hands. It is certainly a theme for rejoicing and congratulation that this beautiful edifice is about to be appropriated to the purposes for which it was erected and opened, ready to receive its cargo of precious human freight here to be prepared and trained for the tempestuous struggle of life. Here the State shall look in future for the educated and trained citizen. From this place there shall come a mighty throng, filled with pure thought, to be governed and directed by a trained and well-stored mind, prepared by their training from the hour they leave the embrace of their Alma Mater to labor for the advancement, the material and moral progress and glory of their State. Upon broad and unsectarian grounds has the University been founded. Springing from the bounty of a great and generous government, where the avenues to greatness are alike open to all, so the doors of this institution are thrown wide open to all. This is as it should be. Science, scholarship, letters, are of no sect. They are of all sects, because they are of humanity itself. To insist upon sectarian education is to insist upon binding the infant mind with an iron cord. No restrained or imprisoned infant grows into the perfect Apollo. Upon the stone seat which Professor Goldwin Smith has placed under a tree of friendly shade in the cool grounds of Cornell University there is an inscription which he wrote, carved in stone: "Above all nations is humanity." It is a text of deathless significance—one which will improve the young minds that will gather there for a hundred years. And here, upon this opening and dedicatory day, let us write for our inscription—aye, let it be carved in imperishable gold upon its gates: "Above all sects, is truth." As the representative of this young Commonwealth, I thus formally confer upon you the authority which appertains to your office as Chancellor of this University. You have been chosen to a high and responsible office, one that will be surrounded with difficulties which may require time to overcome; and yet I take pleasure in assuring you that the confidence which prompted your selection has been strengthened by our acquaintance and association. To you belongs the duty of inaugurating our system of education; to you we entrust the enlightenment of our youth—the beautifying and adorning of those most enduring monuments."

The Chancellor replied briefly in these words:

"With a profound sense of the duties and responsibilities to be assumed, I receive from your hands these symbols of that authority which the Regents have seen fit to bestow upon me. The cordial greetings of your honorable body and that of the people of the State, I return with hearty thankfulness on my own behalf and of the University Faculty. It shall be our earnest endeavor to justify the confidence you have reposed in us, while we shall continue to rely on you for sympathy and unfailing support. Assisted, then, by these skillful and experienced educators, armed with your authority and sustained by your confidence, and relying on the aid of Divine Providence, without which all our labors will be in vain, we enter hopefully on the work to which you have called us."

CHANCELLOR BENTON'S ADDRESS.

The occasion of our assembling to day is one of surpassing dignity and importance. We meet to-day to inaugurate a work whose blessed influence will be felt when the present generation shall have passed away. Though now in its infancy, to-day the University of Nebraska begins to articulate its wishes and its hopes. To-day we celebrate the founding of an institution of learning, in which the best culture of the age may be realized by all. The beneficence of the State has already given it the stamp of an earthly immortality. On the University the State has also inscribed her *own name*, as if anticipating the glory which her University would reflect upon her. No citizen, however wise, virtuous, or patriotic, should supplant the State in such honor. When the temple at Ephesus was burned, Alexander the Great offered to rebuild it, on condition that he be permitted to inscribe his name on the portal tablet. The offer was rejected with disdain as an affront to the city. However much private munificence may supplement the gift of the State, it is eminently fitting that the whole State be represented in the name, as the University is by the people and for the people. All hail! therefore, to the University of Nebraska,—and let us recognize with devout thankfulness that Providence which has led the way to these auspicious beginnings. Let us thank those legislators who with far-seeing wisdom have seized the golden opportunity for establishing a University which may, if rightly fostered, reflect more glory upon the State than all its other achievements. The real glory of a State does not depend so much on its broad and fertile domain, its swarming population, and the activities of industrial life, as on its public and private institutions and the type of manhood which these produce. If this were not so, then China is a more favored land than was Athens, and India should be chosen rather than England. But Athens and England, though pent up in narrow territorial limits, and wrenching subsistence from a reluctant soil, have achieved a place in History, and a name, before which nations, devoid of ennobling institutions, will forever "pale their ineffectual fires." Among these institutions which shed imperishable lustre upon the States that foster them, none rank higher than institutions of learning. To illustrate the dignity that a University gives to a city or nation, permit me to make a historical allusion.

When the city of Leyden, in Holland, was beseiged by a Spanish army, the citizens, inflamed by a love of liberty and religion, made a most desperate resistance. Thousands died by famine and pestilence, and when all other means failed, they opened the dykes, flooded the camp of the enemy, and thus raised the siege, and Holland passed forever from under Spanish rule. As a recompense for their valor, patriotism, and sacrifices, the States' General of Holland gave choice to the city to receive certain exemptions from taxation or to become the site of a new University. Under the advice of one of the heroic defenders of the city, the citizens elected to pay their taxes, and to take their compensation for treasure and life in the establishment of an institution that became the world-renowned University of Leyden.

Through no such toil and suffering have we come to the establishment of a new University in our city and State. Like the manna in the wilderness, it has Providentially fallen into the lap of our prosperity. To us, if rightly used, it will overflow with enriching blessing. Through the munificence of the general government to the State, a grant of valuable land, which we hope to increase by an additional grant, will ultimately place the University in a position of great financial strength, and give it a capacity for usefulness second to none in the land. Having assumed this trust, the State, acting through its legitimate representatives, has built this beautiful structure in which we assemble to-day; and to-day it inaugurates a work, for the intellectual and social culture of the youth of this Commonwealth, upon which we have a right to expect the Divine blessing. Without entering into details, such has been the origin of the endowment and building for the University of Nebraska. This magnificent dowry will detract in no measure, I apprehend, from the virgin charms of this beautiful State; and the supposition may not be too violent, that our emigrating, celibate, *national* Capital may yet desire to unite its fortunes with those of this State and Capital. Whether or not we may have so distinguished a suitor asking to share with us this central home in the national domain, no person of large and comprehensive views, who considers the possibilities of this State, in its position, population and resources, can fail to perceive that the purpose of founding this University evinces the highest wisdom, and that this work is not a superfluity.

But how to organize and administer the University of the State, with all its various colleges, and departments of the several colleges, so as to reach ends that are practical and to meet the essential needs of our times, are questions that occupy and oppress us. If it be becoming at any time to indulge the feeling of modest self-distrust, surely it is proper when standing face to face with these weighty interests and solemn responsibilities. Here is a field large enough for the ambitions of any heart, and a labor which when pushed to the utmost will leave much undone that will appear possible and desirable.

In entering on this work it is highly proper for us to gain if possible a correct idea with regard to what a University is; then we shall be prepared the better to understand its work, its wants and its claims. To these topics we now invite your patient attention, and respectful consideration.

It has been flippantly denied that there are any Universities in America—that the term as applied by us is a misnomer. In the same way, I presume, there is no church in America, because it is not established by law as is that of Russia, England or Prussia. As well say, we have no army, because it is not modeled after any European system. But I think it will be difficult to convince the American public that we have no church, no army: *one* the repository of the religious and moral forces of the nation; the other, the exponent of its physical power and prowess. The *outward* form is not essential to an identity of spirit and character. The States of this nation have long had institutions that justly bear the names of Universities, as this State *intends* to have one. As the spring contains in promise the ripe fruit of autumn, so whatever is in the heart of a free people, will come to ripeness, and mature under the best influence of the nation.

It would be impossible for us to have a University trammeled like foreign ones, with religious tests; patrimonies enjoyed on conditions of maintaining usages that are obsolete or without significance; sinecures filled by men, the fossils of a departed age; and a system of precedents no longer applicable, but adhered to simply because they are precedents.

In the nature of things, our University must harmonize with the genius of our people and the polity of our nation. As governments grow, and are not manufactured, so our educational institutions will express in their form and organization what accords with the genius and wants of our nation.

If we should give but a cursory glance at the development of Universities or higher education in this country, we shall discover that it has had one animating spirit—that has been to fit man for his real life-work.

The antagonism that has been supposed to exist between theory and practice, between men of thought and men of action, is more fancied than real. In the nature of the case, there should be no antagonism. In the mind of God it certainly does not exist. He is both the greatest, the infinite theorizer, and the unwearied worker. In His mind all forms radiant with beauty and order were conceived before they sprang into perfected being. The cosmos of ideas, types or images, were in the Divine thought, cycles of ages, before this majestic order of nature was launched from the plastic hand of the Almighty. I resent the imputation that our higher education has for its purpose or effect a literary delettanteism, which takes the nerve out of a man, and unfits him for practical life.

The first University founded on this Continent was established by clergymen, for the special and technical training of a learned clergy. Hence the motto of Harvard College, "Christo et Ecclesiæ," dedicating the University to Christ and the Church. Soon physicians discovered the practicability and advantage of professional education, and now the *State*—so that we may have no quacks in medicine—forbids the practice of medicine, in most cases, except to such as have obtained their collegiate degree of Bachelor of Medicine.

The learned profession of the law, at first a little slow and conservative, soon after, were inoculated, perhaps by the doctors, with the same ambition for professional training; and within the memory of most of us, the law school has obtained a fine footing, and an amazing fecundity that promises to rival, if not to outstrip its professional competitors.

Following hard after these, and with keen scent for whatever is good, economical, and practicable, "ye modest pedagogue," the modern school master, importunes legislatures until they grant him schools in which he may learn the principles and processes of his art. Though rather slow in recognizing the value of Normal schools for the education of teachers, legislatures have been compelled to make this step *forward*, and teachers intend—nulla vestigia retrorsum—no steps backward. An accomplished preacher who was once asked how he had acquired such skill in his profession, replied—"by ruining half a dozen good congregations."

The day is measurably past when teachers are compelled to ruin schools, in order to learn the methods and principles of their work.

Besides these professional schools, now considered as integral parts of University education, the demand from the industrial classes is heard from every quarter. They also ask for a school master, and like the deep sounding surge that rolls in toward the shore, it is inappeasable and irresistible. This demand of the toiling millions, "who hold communion with nature," in her various forms, was loudest in the very crisis of our nation's peril—the hour of her supreme need. While the youth of our land were drawn from their rural homes to breast the perils of bloody campaigns, that fearfully depleted the ranks of the husbandmen, Congress made haste to bestow on the industrial classes that magnificent endowment for their education contained in the Agricultural College Bill.

Thus a new problem has been forced on educators, the solution of which must be reached slowly, experimentally, and as hitherto, perhaps, with some failures.

But with patience, and honest effort, it will become soundly organized, and take its rank among technical schools, compacted into the general system, and co-ordinated with the other technical schools of the University. The magnitude and complexity of this problem can only be grasped when we take into account the vast number of trades each requiring specific and scientific treatment. They are reckoned by hundreds. To catalogue them would exhaust your patience, and more than exhaust my time.

I have thus glanced hastily at the rise and growth of different departments of education in America, which needs to be understood in order to have a clear conception of what constitutes our University idea. We have spoken of these schools as dissociated and unrelated to each other.

But the economy and symmetry of education, by associating these various departments together, long since became obvious to the practical mind of the nation. Such as are not below the average American, can understand how the same chemist can instruct at once students in medicine, mining, manufactures, and agriculture—how the same apparatus, library, cabinet and museum can serve the wants of all—and especially, where large numbers are gathered into various schools, taught by learned professors, and surrounded by all needful appliances for education, how the spirit of emulation and literary enterprise is awakened, and college life becomes stimulating and vitalizing.

The co-ordinating of these various departments of literary and professional training into one system, sanctioned by one authority, supported by a common fund, under one government, has given form to the American University.

The spirit which animates and vitalizes this form, that binds part to part in kindly, generous sympathy, is the spirit of science. The University embraces with impartial affection every subject; teaches always with reference to "principles;" is ever filled with a scientific spirit; occupies an attitude of scientific inquiry; and offers opportunity and stimulus to all who, in the spirit of scholars, will "scorn delights and live laborious days."

In this brief expose, we have aimed to indicate the corporate form and animating spirit of the American University.

II. In the next place, it is desirable to gain, if possible, definite conceptions of the proper functions of the University. This implies an inquiry into the *ends* for which education is undertaken, and the *means* by which it may be accomplished.

If we inquire with regard to the *ends* of liberal culture, or any culture, we are met at the very threshold of our investigation by a fact, which like the thread of Ariadne, will guide us through all the mazes of this intricate labyrinth. That fact is, there is a *destiny*, or law of unfolding, that is appointed to every created, progressive being.

This law affords an unerring clue to the discovery of every truth; and, is also, a certain test by which we may try every educational theory.

From the acorn, nothing but the oak can be produced. The destiny of the acorn, in its form and structure, is an oak—not a willow or a pine tree. As culture cannot change its essential character, so all culture should aim to give it grander, statelier proportions, as an oak.

In animal life the same principle holds true. The eagle's egg can only produce the eaglet. No care in the incubation can hatch from it an owl or a goose; no skill in training can rear our national bird so as to mouse for its prey in twilight, or to become a swimmer of the waters.

So with man; he has his preordained relations and duties—in a word, his destiny, to which his development, or education, should conduct him most directly.

Education, then, has for its proper end, not some *ideal*, rounding out of a system; not the attainment of some theoretic harmony of the elements of manhood; but such an unfolding as will enable him to fill in the highest measure that destiny to which he has been preordained.

At birth man is introduced into three great circles of relations. These circles are concentric, the common center of which is the infant human being. The first circle includes his relations to Nature; the second, his relations to Society; and the third, his relations to the Infinite, to the Spiritual, to God. This broad and exhaustive generalization states all the possibilities and requirements of a human being. A most powerful living writer of fiction, Victor Hugo, has unfolded, with surpassing interest and effect, these three great classes of relation—man's relation to nature, in his Toilers of the Sea; his relations to society, in his Les Miserables; and his relations to God, in his Notre Dame.

The all-embracing mind of Shakspeare has embodied substantially the same grand classification in the well-known address of Cardinal Woolsey:

> Let ALL the ends thou aimest at, be thy Country's, thy God's and Truth's.

God, Society, and Truth—these are the all-comprehending aims of life.

If these relations and duties are in ever-widening circles, how insensate and irrational, that education which ignores or denies them. Blinder than a mole is that educator who will circumscribe all the labors and knowledge of the student to the narrow circle of nature. This is the very dry rot that eats out all strength, or comeliness, from our system of education. Instead of lifting the mind to contemplate a millenium of knowledge, which takes hold of humanity and divinity, the apostles of materialism, like Buckle and Herbert Spencer, teach a millenium of corn and bacon. To them, that knowledge is worth most which enables a man to make the best living. While this is, without doubt, the first in the order of nature, it is not first in order of importance. This materialistic, so-called practical education, is that which man shares with the brutes. The lower animals, like man, have activities that lead to self-preservation, the care of offspring, and forming a social community. The dignity and importance of human education must, therefore, be in some other direction. The value of our civilization does not consist in the increase of facilities for supporting man's animal life, or in giving a keener relish to human existence. If man's destiny could be fully realized, in what ministers to his physical existence and enjoyment, then the *great*, the *only* question would be, what shall we eat? what shall we drink? and wherewithal shall we be clothed? But we all instinctively feel that such a destiny, and the education for such a destiny as *this*, fall infinitely below man's conscious dignity and capabilities.

Confess that your rule of life is simply to make a living, and you confess that you would eliminate every noble and generous sentiment from your heart. Said a *thieving* miscreant once to Talleyrand, in apology for his offence: "One must *live*, you know." In reply, the caustic Frenchman said: "I confess I do not see the *necessity*."

Life is a matter of infinite litttleness, an abortive attempt of creative intelligence, if it must forever be "cabined, cribbed, confined," to the narrow round of sensuous pursuits and gratifications.

But in addition to this, let human society appear, with its complex relations of child, parent, teacher, neighbor, friend, and citizen, with all their related industries in social, commercial, and political organizations. Here a new and broader field opens before us, and a new education, made necessary, to fit man for his new circumstances and duties. Among the ancients, it was held of first importanee that every child should be trained to be a worthy member of the State. Though Socrates was a statuary by trade, and thus earned his livelihood, his imperishable fame rests not on enriching the world by his art, but on teaching the youth what were their duties to society and the gods. This branch of education, though confessedly more difficult to conduct successfully, than merely intellectual training, is not impracticable. Common sense says a man may be educated for *society* as well as for *science*. The cultivated, the polite, the graceful man of the world—the orator, the patriot, the statesman, are entities, recognized by our language as the products and legitimate results of training and education. These—one and all—may be uninfluenced by the celestial light and attractions which lift the soul to acts of self-denying heroism and fortify it to bear with solid patience the painful toils of life, or to gain th honors of martyrdom. Whatever may be the inspiring idea, man can be trained by education in the moral sentiments to love truth and justice; to love liberty and right, country and man, and especially to have a broad, generous, cosmopolitan sympathy with humanity itself, which shall so weld the soul to the race as to make it the sharer of its toils as well as of its triumph.

When this line from Terence was recited in the Roman theater: "Homo sum; humani nihil a me alienum puto"—I am a man, and indifferent to nothing which pertains to man—the whole theater rose to its feet, shouting its tumultuous applause; and, the human heart everywhere swells with admiration and approval of the philanthropy of that noble sentiment. It is the second essential of Christianity—it takes us back to Nazareth itself.

But the best, the broadest arena for human thought is not man in his physical or social relations, but in his relations to the infinite, to God. Science, in its last analysis, brings us to God. The last word of social science is God. This word solves mysteries, dissipates doubts and establishes man in earnest convictions.

When Schelling, the great German philosopher, who, his whole life, having been tossed on the waves of speculation and doubt, was asked at the very close of his life of unrest, what was the highest generalization of science, replied in the words of an apostle: "OF Him, i. e., God, are all things, BY Him are all things, and FOR Him are all things." God, the source, the upholding power, and the final end of all created things.

As we heve seen, there are difficulties in the way of imparting an education in *social* duties, so the obstacles in the way of religious culture are still greater.

If, therefore, this be a segment in a true and complete system of education, the question arises, what can the University do in such a matter? Can the State have anything to do with religion?

Here, I know, we tread on delicate and debateable ground; and yet, it seems to me, that the practical solution of this question is not so formidable as the theoretical difficulties imply. Nor, do I propose, with moral cowardice, to thrust this matter out of sight, that it may be out of mind. Is it true that education in our Universities founded by the State, must be Atheistic—without God? Such has been the opinion of some otherwise right-minded men, who echo the sentiments of theorists, without observing facts as they exist before our face. An Atheistic school shocks the moral sense of the whole people, and in our country is an unpardonable anomaly. While the University has nothing to do with "*isms*," however reputable by age or the number of their adherents, she must always be interested in truth, and all truth is permeated with the idea of God. History, science, literature, mind, matter, all are interpenetrated with this idea, and to ignore it, the University must ignore the most momentous truths and facts, and be a stranger to the celestial motives, and divine love, that must warm the soul before it can rise from being an erratic meteor, to be a grand planetary soul shining with steady stellar lustre in the firmament of infinite blessedness.

The average religious character of our people is such, that they will demand a distinct and an unequivocal recognition, in the daily exercises of their University, of the practical principles of our common Christianity; and thus the University will simply reflect the average religious character of our people

It is also worthy of note, that the most devout of our educated men are most likely to be interested in education; and by some general law of affinity, are attracted to this kind of labor. Thus, it happens, that the whole business of education is fragrant with heavenly odors. As those, who make the voyage to India, are regaled by delicious perfumes, wafted from "Araby the blest," so those, who shall travel up the hill of science, shall be refreshed as by perfumes from the garden of the Lord.

In as concise a manner as possible, I have endeavored to show that the proper end of education is threefold, to fit man for his relations to nature, to society and to God.

We are thus naturally brought to the question—what means, or what studies will conduce to the attainment of such ends? What should our youth be taught, in order, to use the words of Milton, that they may be fitted for all spots and crises; qualified to perform magnanimously, skilfully and justly, all the affairs, both public and private, of peace and war; inflamed with the love of learning, and the admiration of virtue; stirred up by hopes of living to be brave men and worthy patriots, dear to God and famous to all ages.

In prescribing a course of study, two things should be steadily kept in view: First—The imparting of knowledge; second—The discipline of the faculties. These are the distinctive objects of a liberal education.

In the impartation of knowledge, it certainly does not come within the scope of the University to teach the arts and trades of life. It will teach the facts and principles on which all arts and trades rest. Instead of teaching the elements of knowledge applicable to some craft or art, by which a livelihood may be made, it will unfold principles with such a scientific spirit as to lead most directly and easily to artizan or professional skill. Liberal education is not professional education. The one should precede the other. The former is needed to make men; the latter to perfect them in some branch of human industry. These are the results reached by comprehensive and protracted experimenting in education, and may not readily be set aside, or destroyed by educational Philistines.

Nor would I be understood to say, that there is no other possible way of achieving the proper ends of education, than by such a system as now obtains in our higher institutions of learning. By no means. But only this: that they adopt the *shortest*, most *certain*, and most *effective* means ot reaching the proper results of liberal culture. But out of this infinite whole, in which all knowledge is contained, what selection should be made, adapted to the purposes of the teacher as a trainer of men?

This question is eminently an experimental one. Were we to classify human knowledge, it would be sufficiently exact for our present purpose, to say, that all is embraced in a knowledge of *mind* and of *matter*.

The science of mind embraces whatever belongs to the history of man, as a thinking, speaking, social, acting being. Hence, as a thinking being, he will be studied with respect to the laws of thought and the principles of taste in the fine arts; as a speaking being, the acquisition of language as the *form* of thought, and the study of literature, luminous and creative, as the store-house of all that the race has thought, the daguerreotype of its mental progress, will claim the attention of the scholar. As a social being the organization of States, the principles of law, civil polity, political economy, and the whole history of man in his migrations, with all the social upheavals and subsidences of the race, would form a part in a comprehensive system of liberal culture. As language, in the words of Humboldt, is the *outward* appearance of the intellect of nations, so institutions embody the social instincts and experience of the race. If the study of mankind is the most appropriate work for man, then these branches of learning may not be omitted.

If we turn to the other department of knowledge—the realm of matter—there is no dissent as to what should be studied in a liberal course of education. The utility of the knowledge of those sciences which add to the comfort or adornment of life is scarcely called in question, and hardly needs illustration. In the "New Education," as it is called, these studies are chief, and most highly prized. In all the stirring activities of life—the commerce, the manufactures and agriculture of the civilized world, science has worked amazing revolutions, augmenting in a tenfold degree the capacity of material nature to contribute to the well-being of man.

It is not our purpose to discuss the relative advantage of these different departments of human knowledge, nor yet to consider the *manner* or the *extent* each should be pursued; but simply to show that they have an adaptation to the intellectual and physical wants of man, and an imperishable interest for all ages. Hence, I must here commend the wise judgment and generous liberality of the Regents of the University, who aim to secure to every University student instruction in any branch of knowledge; and at the same time, to afford him "room and verge" enough to select such branches as most accord with his taste and life-work; and which, at the same time, will give that intellectual and moral discipline that he will need as a man. With this hasty sketch of the outline of a liberal education, we pass to some concluding observations on the wants of a University.

First—The most pressing want of all our Universities is the want of money. The oldest of the Universities in the United States are just as clamorous to-day for an increase of funds as are those recently founded. Harvard University, the oldest, whose endowment is generally regarded as munificent, of which *individual donations* form a large part, is prevented by lack of funds from accomplishing all that a University should do.

Of Yale, a Professor of that college says: "The Professors are not half paid—the salaries are not more than half sufficient to support a family respectably in New Haven—the corps of instructors ought to be doubled. She has not a dollar to buy books." These are but samples of the oldest and the richest colleges in our land. They teach us an important lesson, that for University education there must be a concentration of funds and no division of them. Hence, we can really have but *one* State University.

This work is too expensive for individual efforts, but may appropriately be supplemented by the generous gifts of patriotic citizens.

The State has appropriately assumed this responsibility, and will find occasion from time to time, to increase the resources of the University, by appropriations that will be inconsiderable, when compared with expenditures made for far less worthy objects.

Second—In the next place, the University needs efficient supervision and the sanction of public authority. The men who stand behind the faculty, and who hold the reins of power, can, if partizan or malicious, ruin the University. The State has, therefore, wisely lodged this supervisory and controling power in a Board of Regents, and such control wisely conditioned, is one of the prime elements of our University success. Selected to this special work and responsibility, they are more likely to be intelligent, capable, and deeply interested in educational work, than if charged with this supervision as an appendage to other more exacting official duties. The flourishing condition of Universities in adjoining States, under the control of a special Board, admonishes us to hold fast that which is good. Nor is it needful for me here to say anything to increase your confidence in the men who have, with sagacity and prudence thus far, directed the affairs of the University, as they are not strangers to you, but known to all as practical and sagacious, and above all, keenly alive to everything that concerns the honor or the prosperity of the University.

Third—Again, the University has some right to ask for patience from the citizens of the State. In the work of intellectual training, it is impossible to sow and reap in the same day. You have a right to expect constant progress, enlargement, improvement; but we cannot spring into being with the prestige and accumulated resources of some of the older Universities, at the waving of any magic wand, however potent. Our work is a growth; but give the University of Nebraska the years you give our youth to come to their majority, and she will rival in her learned Professors, in her elegant buildings, her laboratory, libraries, cabinets, works of art, and museum, and above all, and supporting all, in her munificent endowment, the most favored University of all these States. These are not the words of flattery and adulation, but are certain to come to their fulfillment, if the wise forecast of the founders of the University shall be properly seconded by the succession of Boards of Regents, Chancellors and Faculty, reaching through a series of years, supported by the sympathy and co-operation of the State. This immense work will always require ceaseless vigilance, exhaustless patience, and often a lofty and daring courage, that sees no obstacles. In that great naval battle, in which Admiral Nelson lost his life, Lord Collingwood reported that some of the British ships were retreating. With splendid mockery of fear Nelson raised his telescope to his *sightless* eye, and quickly remarked, "I do not see it. Give command to sail in." This kind of heroism, that

> " Holds no parley with unmanly fears,
> But where duty points, confidently steers,"

will often need to be called into play, in the various emergencies of our University growth and development. In view of all the known obstacles to the realization of our ideal of a University, to bring it rapidly to that condition of development and influence at which we aim, I most earnestly entreat for patience and favorable interpretation of our acts from all citizens.

Speaking for the faculty, and including truly as I believe, you, gentlemen of the Board of Regents, it is no unmeaning word to say to this audience that we all have our qualification for our positions—a profound sense of the importance, responsibility and difficulty of our work. With proper self-distrust, which shall lead us prayerfully to seek that wisdom that cometh from above, we all enter with good purpose and heart into this University work.

FOURTH—And lastly, in our partial and imperfect sketch of University wants, it would be a beggarly account which makes no mention of students. To-day we open the University, without a class, without a student enrolled. But for those who shall honor themselves by being the first class to enrol themselves to-morrow as students of the University, I have a word. You have the faith and courage to come to this new University, trusting its future. The success and reputation of the University are largely in your hands. Your faithfulness and student zeal will give us a good name abroad, induce hundreds to come, and thus compel our rapid enlargement in means of instruction. Or, by idleness, insubordination and neglect, you may seriously injure all. Dr. Thomas Arnold once said to the Rugby boys: "It is not necessary to have a hundred students here, but it is necessary that those who are here shall be gentlemen." So I say to-day, we do not need a hundred, but we need men and women You are here to make the University, as well as to be made. By your noble and manly conduct here, you will bear an honored part in building this University, of which, *some* will hereafter be Regents or Professors, and in which *all* may have an honest pride. Young men and young women, we welcome you both alike to the toils, responsibilities and triumphs of our University life.

On this Autumn day, long to be held in memory, as the Autumn sun declines in the west, the crescent glory of a new fountain of intellectual light takes its place in the firmament of literature and science. As a ship, it begins to glide over the water, well manned, rejoicing in its bounding life, its canvass full spread, and every heart beating with joy and hope of a prosperous voyage. Speaking for the Regents, the Faculty, students, and all represented in this work, I say, God bless the ship; God bless the builders; God bless the picked crew; and not to be forgotten, God bless all the passengers.

J. STERLING MORTON'S ADDRESS.

As men have rendered immortal their lives, and names, by great thoughts, or great deeds, so days have become historical and their annual recurrence been made the occasion of congratulation and thanksgiving, because of the great events of which they have been the mothers.

Nebraska, seventeen years ago last May, became an organized Territory of the United Statess, by virtue of Congressional enactment. In January of the year 1855, her Territorial Legislature assembled for the first time, and in 1867 she became a State in the Federal Union. These events were important, and will be forever commemorated in the history of the country. But this day is coequal in importance with any in our brief civil life of little more than half a generation.

This day inaugurates the University of the State of Nebraska. The United States founded this institution upon the substantial basis of a munificent grant of land. It was born with the State. It is coexistent with it. While the State stands the University must remain. The endless legacy, the magnificent heritage which has been set apart, sacred to and solely and indivertably for its maintenance, makes it as permanent and indestructable as the commonwealth itself. This is the school of the people. They are its trustees. They are its regents. They cannot utterly destroy it. They may dwarf, but they cannot kill. And they should foster, and tone, and energize it to a growth which shall render it equal to any, and excelled by no college in America. The people, properly understanding and fully appreciating the use and benefits of this University, not only to the generation in which we live, but to the millions which are to follow us in the quick journey from the cradle to the grave, can make; will make it their especial care and pride, and so doing, will discharge their duty to their country, to their children, and to their God.

Americans declare that all men must be educated, because the American Government is founded in the intelligence of its citizens. We believe that education is as necessary to the development of a human being mentally, as is food, and air, and water, and light to his physical growth and existence.

An illiterate and uneducated people are not capable of self government; therefore, the perfecting of educational systems, which shall embrace all the citizens, and shed knowledge upon all the people as fully and impartially as the sun its light, is the only legitimate method of perpetuating the Republic.

Our school system is for facility divided into four parts. The primary, which takes the pupil through the district or common school; the union or high school, which prepares him for the University; and the University, which disciplines him for the battle of life, and, its departments of agriculture, mechanic arts, law and medicine, will fit him for specific duties and responsibilities in that conflict.

The Normal school, the sole object of which is to prepare trained teachers for the primary schools, is as essential as the departments of the University, and should meet with the greatest kindness and consideration at the hands of every citizen who thinks.

All the parts are in unison, like the machinery of a well regulated timepiece, and together, by their success or failure, will indicate the intelligence and prosperity of this people as accurately and unmistakably as the hands upon the dial-plate tell the hours of the day.

The Normal school sustains the primary; the primary the high school; the high school the University; and the University vitalizes the State with learning, furnishing scholars for her law-makers, and men of mental strength and training for governors and her judges. Thus the State itself, and its dignity, and prosperity, and honor, depends upon the success of our system of education.

To maintain and energize it, we have endowed it with a landed estate equal to a kingdom. For its constant and steady labors, we provide money, by taxation, upon all the people. We have thus opened the doors to the children of the State, and tendered them free entry and welcome while tarrying within the temples of knowledge.

There may be some whose parents will deprive them of this privilege, either through carelessness, or through prejudice, which is the child of ignorance. And to guard against such deprivation, and to fully complete and round out this educational system, we must have laws which shall compel the attendance at some school, either private or public, of all the children in Nebraska. We have given land and paid money to the State to the end that education may be universal, and may we not demand laws that shall secure the end?

The parent who maims the body of his child, who maltreats and deforms his offspring, is made answerable to the law, and is sent to prison. And if the State takes such care of the bodies of the children, and punishes those who abuse them, may it not with still greater propriety, take care of and prevent the dwarfing, the maiming, and mutilating of their immortal souls, through ignorance, enforced by ignorant or wicked parents?

The strength of the Republic is in the intelligence of the people; to disseminate intelligence is simply to perpetuate this Government, and therefore, laws compelling the attendance at school of all children, are nothing more, nothing less, than wholesome laws, looking to and securing the permanency of the American Union.

Who will oppose such legislation? What argument shall be brought to put it down, and by what cowards and demagogues shall it be uttered?

It is not to thinking and reading men a new idea. It was a living thought, and animating great actions, three hundred years before the birth of Christ. According to Plutarch, Alexander the Great, when he had led his resistless legions against the Scythians and all Asia was subject to him, profoundly studied how his authority and the laws of Greece should best be maintained when he was at a distance. And to secure this object, Alexander selected thirty thousand boys, and gave them masters to instruct them in Grecian literature. Here, then, was compulsory education, enforced upon the children of a conquered people, not as a punishment, but to teach them the superiority of

Grecian civilization, and of the laws, customs, and literature of the Athenians, so that they, too, might be inspired with a love of them, and they, too, become truly men of Athens.

Not any battles with the Barbarians, not all the conflicts with the Persians nor the conquest of the armies of Darius, nor his magnanimity to the captive family of that monarch, entitled Alexander to be called "the Great," so much as did the enforcement of education upon the up-growing intellect of a nation which he had made subject to his own. He knew that knowledge would wean humanity from barbarism, and that education alone could support the supreme acy and glory of Greece.

The idea of compulsory education was alive then, and it lives to-day. It was practical then as a means of maintaining a government, and it is equally practical to-day for the same purpose.

But we are told our schools may become sectarian or denominational. This is a vain fear and groundless. The highways of knowledge are in no more danger of becoming denominationalized than are the highways of commerce, and no sane man objects to the Burlington and Missouri River Railroad for fear it may become a Congregational railroad, nor to the Union Pacific for fear it may get to be a Methodist, or a Baptist, or Presbyterian, or Roman Catholic or Episcopalian railroad.

As the highways of travel and commerce are the servitors of the people, and the purveyors to their physical comfort and material welfare, without sectarian bias or influence, so shall our public schools, the highways leading to knowledge, be the unsectarian mental servitors of the citizens, and trainers of the popular mind, developing our intellectual resources and capacities, just as railroads do our material wealth.

And while our public schools are unsectarian, they shall be not un-American. To be American, they will be not denominational, nor partizan, nor must they foment or perpetuate political discord. On the other hand, they should inspire a love of country, a pride of nationality, broad as our plains, inculcate integrity, solid and enduring as our mountains, and teach that the true greatness of the American people will be best demonstrated by the learning, the honesty, the temperance and morality of their leading statesmen. To awaken in every youthful mind the grandest impetus to honorable life, a love of America, a love of liberty regulated by law, and a reverence for learning, a devotion to truth, and a sincere and simple faith in that Majestic Mentality which marks alike the planet's course and the sparrow's fall, is the true office of the American school. Thus imperfectly we have come to the theme of the dignity of the office of teacher.

The office to which attaches, in a Republican form of Government, the greatest responsibilities is that of parent. The greatest influence upon the Republic is wielded from that position, and wielded, too, by woman, enjoying alone the God-given rights of the highest, gravest, and most holy office—MOTHER!

The Queens of England form not one tenth so much the laws of that country, direct not one-tenth so much its industries and prosperities, mental and material, as do the mothers—our American Queens—in moulding the mental and moral character of their sons and daughters of the United States.

Next after this office in influence of enduring and self-perpetuating character, in dignity and grave responsibility, comes the office of the American teacher. His it is to labor, during life, in the diffusion of knowledge, the spread of intelligence among the people, who are the government.

He who could for a generation stop the schools of this Republic, close up the avenues to learning, and drive the teachers into banishment, would have effectually subverted the government of the people.

The education, universal education of Americans, is the blood, and breath, and the bone and sinew, and soul of the Republic. The office of those men and women, whose duty it is to breathe the life of knowledge, the vitality of education into a self-governing people of forty millions of souls, is worthy of the exaltation, and should command the highest consideration of every thinker in all this broad and beautiful land.

The teacher makes his mental mark upon an individual pupil to-day; to-morrow that pupil, himself a teacher, rewrites on a hundred human minds the influence and character of that first instructor.

In two generations, the ideas, the mental habits and characteristics of a single teacher in a primary school, will have seized upon and permeated a million of sentient beings. This result is inevitable.

It is as certain that the intellectual, and moral character of the teacher shall make its impress upon the mind of the pupil, as that the sunlight shall write your correct image in the camera and make it your photograph.

The office of teacher reaches forward into the remotest future, and, handling the viewless machinery of mind, forms governments, and moulds civilizations yet unborn.

The architect plans and constructs temples and palaces in solid masonry, and with iron and with wood, rears aloft our public edifices—monuments to his own skill, and a reflex of the intellectuality of the age in which he lives. This beautiful and symmetrical building is his work. Long may it stand, usefully may it flourish for generations!

We call his office one of gravity and responsibility, yet it is only the grouping, mapping together, in form and true proportion, of such rough and perishable things as brick and mortar.

But the teacher, who within these walls, plans the mental strength of the people, who maps here the young and vigorous intellect of this young and vigorous State, is the architect who carves out of individual minds, skilled in knowledge, and adapted, each to its place, the temples of good government and of civil and religious liberty. These edifices will crumble, and their very dust be carried away by the winds. But the architecture of the mentality of the commonwealth, which here shall have been given solidity and symmetry, shall endure forever and ever. It will influence and ornament the ages to come, and finally become a part of the imperishable structures of the house not made with hands, which fadeth not away—eternal in the heavens. The profession of the teacher is fraught with responsibilities, and interwoven with duties of such dignity that it spans the valley and shadow of death as with a bridge which crosses up to the judgment seat of God Himself.

Those who adopt it should be pure men and women, realizing the magnitude of the eternal responsibilities which it entails. Far-reaching as to the last mortal that shall be born upon earth, high-aspiring as the pearly gates beyond the stars, the influence of the teacher is coexistent with mind itself.

Two hundred and forty years before the Christian Era, Cato discoursed upon the exalted position of the teacher, and amid his manifold duties as Censor of Rome, "took upon himself the office of schoolmaster to his own son, though he had a slave named Chilo, who was a good grammarian, and taught several other children." But the noble Roman tells us that he did not choose that his son should be reprimanded by a slave, or that he should be indebted to so mean a person for his education. He was, therefore, (says Plutarch) himself his preceptor in grammar, and in law, and wrote histories for him with his own hands, in large characters, that, without stirring out of his father's house, he might gain a knowledge of the great actions of the ancient Romans, and of the customs of his country.

Surely we in the nineteenth century should be able to see, in our light, clearly the dignity of that office which Cato so revered and honored, by accepting, even in the dim light of the misty morning time of human knowledge; before yet the letters of the alphabet had began their tireless labors of sowing thoughts broadcast, up and down the mental fallow-fields of all the world.

The sculptor who wakes from formless sleep in the solid marble the statue or exact image of the poet, the philosopher, or the statesman, attains fame; and such as Powers, and Mills, and Randolph Rogers, among Americans, we cherish with national pride. Their works stand pre-eminent among the adornments of the National Capital, and there Columbus, the discoverer, Washington, the founder, Jackson, the defender, Lincoln, the protector, breathe again in their marble counterfeits.

The work of the statuary approximates what men call immortality more nearly than any other materialistic labor.

Phidias, the Athenian sculptor, whose sublime conceptions were wrought in the ornaments of the Parthenon, and many of which are at this day preserved among the marbles of the British Museum, achieved perhaps the most lasting fame of any of the ancient statuaries. He lived and executed its works more than two thousand years ago, and this is longevity even for marble men. But the American teacher, even in our common schools, is a sculptor, whose works, in the undying marble of human mentality, shall outlive the stone images of the Greek and the Roman; these mental images will loom up among the statesmen and benefactors of our race forever, reflecting and immortalizing the genius of those who carved, and shaped, and toned them in the plastic days of youth in the studies of the schools.

The American educator carves a statuary out of the minds of the youth whom he instructs, which is co-immortal with the soul itself, a statuary which shall always stand in the pantheon of our country's history, and at last, its symmetry, and beauty, and perfection be examined in the light of eternity, by Him who first carved the mental man in the image of the Divine mind.

The schoolmaster, in the humblest school building in Nebraska, is quietly but certainly, developing a statuary which shall outlive Parian marble and time itself—a statuary, which through the endless cycles of eternity, either in Heaven or in hell, shall attest his fidelity to his trust, and his comprehension of the vastness and delicacy of the work he has undertaken.

We demand for Nebraska educated educators. We demand professional, trained Teachers; men and women of irreproachable character, and well-tested abilities. We demand from our legislature, laws raising the standard of the profession and exalting the office of the teacher.

As the doctor of medicine or the practicioner at law is only admitted within the pale of his calling upon the production of his parchment or certificates, so the applicant for the position of instructor in our primary and other schools, should be required by law to first produce his diploma, his authority to teach from the Normal Schools.

We call no uneducated quack or charlatan, to perform surgery upon the bodies of our children lest they may be deformed, crippled and maimed physically all their lives. Let us take equal care that we intrust the development of the mental faculties to skilled instructors, of magnanimous character, that the mentalities of our children may be not mutilated, deformed, and crippled to halt and limp through all the centuries of their never ending lives. The deformed body will die, and be forever put out of our sight under the ground, but a mind made monstrous by bad teaching, dies not but stalks forever among the ages, an immortal mockery of the Divine Image!

The compensation for the services of a proficient teacher in the primary schools should be equal to that of a competent physician or lawyer, or minister of the gospel. His salary should be sufficient to command all of his time, all of his abilities, all of his efforts, and relieve him of any concern whatever, as to his decent and comfortable maintenance.

The professor in the High Schools, the University, and the Normal School should be paid so well that the best educators of the union may be attracted, as they have been, to our employ, and personally interested in the educational development of the State.

The people in every country should be alive and sensitive to the care of their schools, and to the fact that this University offers free access to the higher walks of science wherein the youth of Nebraska may attain the highest honors and distinction.

If these facts be appreciated, if these precious advantages be improved, thirty years from to-day the Alumni of this institution will have made their impress for the good, the true and the ennobling upon every statute law in the State, upon every school district in every county; and the ripened fruits of this system of education will cluster richly in the legislative, executive, and judicial departments of the entire Commonwealth.

Here is free education.

The emoluments of the instructors depend not upon the number of students nor the number who graduate in any of the departments. The honors of the University of Nebraska, because money does not buy them, will be all the more sacred. He who gets a degree here must pay for it in honest, worthy ambitious weeks and months and years of mental toil. The people demand, genuinely earned diplomas and their standard of requirements will be high as the endowment and support of the institution is broad and liberal.

Not family influence nor partizan power shall here pluck unearned honors. Only true mental merit and honest effort shall here receive the laurels.

To graduate from the University of Nebraska shall be an honor among her people even now, and the day is not distant when her Diploma shall be at par with those of Yale, Union, Harvard, and the University of Michigan, all over the world of Literature and of Art.

As in ancient Rome, the gates of Janus were thrown open to indicate existing war, so to-day we open wide the doors of the University of the State of Nebraska, as a token of perpetual, organized, systematized war against ignorance and bigotry and intolerance and vice in every form among the people of this State and the youth who in a few fleeting years, will become its legislators, its judges and its governors.

To the good citizens of the city of Lincoln is committed the formation of the society and influences which shall immediately surround the social life of this school. They must remember that as disease is infectious, and good health never, and only preserved by temperate living and good habits, so evil habits are contagious and pure character only protected by pure associations. Upon them much of the success and influence of this institution depends, for they can by municipal regulations as to the youth of the State who shall here assemble, answer in some degree that supreme supplication of the Lord's Prayer, "Deliver us from evil, Lead us not into temptation."

Every good man and woman who lives here should make it an especial study and a sleepless duty to render the social and moral atmosphere of the student pleasant and pure, and if this be accomplished the prosperity and usefulness of the University has received a help which no man can estimate and your city a blessing which no mere material prosperity can secure.

Mr. Chancellor, and Gentlemen of the Faculty of the University of Nebraska:

As a citizen of this youthful and sturdy State it affords me the sincerest satisfaction to welcome you in the name of all the people to the high and honorable duties of your responsible positions; and in doing this I am permitted also to congratulate you most heartily upon the fact that public sentiment throughout the State is united in friendship for this most beneficent enterprize. Neither political nor denominational prejudice dares utter one word to dishearten or weaken that sentiment. The whole soul of the State breathes aspirations for your prosperity and usefulness.

One of the grandest of material labors is the reduction of untried lands to tillage. Here upon these timberless plains for sixteen years, in nurseries and in gardens, intelligent industry has been growing trees, until now new forests are waving in the winds and rich foliage is shimmering in the sunlight where then was the blank monotony of prairies. Savants believe that these groves have changed the climate, and experience confirms in us their faith. We know that our winters are less rigorous and our summers less arid and oppressive, and timber out of which to construct buildings more abundant. To-day all over the State in our school houses we are germinating mental men and women, they are being cultivated in our educational nurseries; soon they will be transplanted by you and trained into a higher growth and more stately proportions, and thus shall our moral and intellectual climate be ripened and refined and the timber out of which to construct a strong State become more abundant.

But while the tillage of this bountiful soil brings forth fruit that perishes, the cultivation of mind in which you engage, will yield fruit as imperishable as the rewards and penalties of eternity itself. As now, leaves and the fruit are falling in the orchard, preparatory to the icy sleep of winter, and we have faith that in the early summer time, under the genial sunshine, there will again come buds and bloom and fruit; so you are assured that, though the pupils you instruct will pass from the summer of youth to the autumn of age, and at last sink into the winter of the grave; there is an immortal spring time coming, an Eternal summer, when—God grant it!—your careful culture shall bear fruits of inestimable worth and unfading beauty. Every instructor should be constantly conscious that he has adopted that calling which was made high and honorable more than eighteen hundred years ago by that Divine Teacher whom God ordained to begin the education of the world. Every true educator must remember that his high exemplar is He who taught as never man taught—who imparted that profound wisdom, that sublime knowledge which has been to mankind a consecration, that Teacher by the "spiritual splendor of whose Being the ages have been lighted upward forever," and in whose look and precept and action, were supreme dignity, and beauty, and charity, and infinite consolation.

Letter from President Ira Mayhew.

DETROIT, MICHIGAN, August 29, 1871.

DEAR SIR:—Sincerely regretting my inability to attend the inaugural exercises of the University of Nebraska on the 6th of September, I yet rejoice that so many of our newer States are like yours, laying broad and sure foundations for future greatness in providing so amply for both common schools and higher education. The manifest tendency at the present time to conform courses of study to the prospective wants of students, I believe to be an indication of greater good to coming generations than is now generally appreciated. Many progressive educators, I doubt not, are building better than they are aware. Young men will better take culture when studying with a specfic object in view, than when they have no well laid plans to work out, or high purpose to fulfill. I hope and trust, sir, you may be able to build well for the youth of Nebraska, and for the early and permanent greatness of the State. Regretting my inability to be present with the friends of popular education on so auspicious an occasion, that I might personally tender to you my congratulations,

I am, dear sir, faithfully yours,

IRA MAYHEW.

HON. A. R. BENTON, Lincoln. Nebraska.

Letter from Hon. Geo. H. Pendleton.

CINCINNATI, OHIO, August 30, 1871.

A. R. BENTON, ESQ., Chancellor, etc.:

My Dear Sir:—I have to acknowledge the receipt of your polite invitation to be present at the inauguration exercises of the University of Nebraska, on the 6th of September.

I regret that I am constrained to forego the pleasure. An acceptance would add greatly to the interest of a visit which I have long desired to make to your State. We can scarcely realize that you are about to inaugurate a University munificently endowed, in a State which so lately attained to the dignity even of a territorial government. It is a striking illustration of the fact so full of satisfaction to the patriot as well as the philanthropist, that everywhere in our country, institutions of learning and religion keep well apace with the footsteps of our race. I trust the University of Nebraska will be eminently successful and that its career will be as useful to the future generations as its foundation is honorable to this.

I am, very repectfully,

GEO. H. PENDLETON.

Letter from Hon. Wm. Bross.

TRIBUNE EDITORIAL ROOMS,
CHICAGO, September 4, 1871.

HON. J. STERLING MORTON:

My Dear Sir:—I have to acknowledge with many thanks the receipt of an invitation to attend "The inaugural exercises of the University of Nebraska," on September 6. I regret very much that my other engagements will render it impossible for me to attend. I beg to assure you, however, of the deep interest I take in the progress and the prosperity of your noble State. The establishment of a University at so early a day in your history is worthy of all praise and has my best wishes for its abundant success.

Very truly, your ob't servant,

WM. BROSS.

www.ingramcontent.com/pod-product-compliance
Lightning Source LLC
LaVergne TN
LVHW011140110826
845150LV00008B/2432

* 9 7 8 1 4 1 8 1 9 2 8 8 4 *